Reliquary

POEMS

Matthew Minicucci

Accents Publishing ◆ Lexington KY ◆ 2013

Copyright © 2013 by Matthew Minicucci
All rights reserved

Printed in the United States of America

Accents Publishing
Editor: Katerina Stoykova-Klemer
Designer: Simeon Kondev
Cover Illustration: Jacopo Bellini, *Christ in the Grave*

Accents Publishing is an independent press for brilliant voices. For a catalog of current and upcoming titles, please visit us on the Web at http://www.accents-publishing.com

ISBN: 978-1-936628-13-1
First Edition
10 9 8 7 6 5 4 3 2 1

For My Classmates

Contents

Figure 1: Jesus Is Condemned to Death/1
Figure 2: Jesus Takes Up His Cross/2
Figure 3: Jesus Falls (1)/4
Figure 4: Jesus Meets His Mother/6
Figure 5: Simon of Cyrene/8
Figure 6: Veronica Wipes the Face of Jesus/10
Figure 7: Jesus Falls (2)/11
Figure 8: The Women of Jerusalem Weep/13
Figure 9: Jesus Falls (3)/14
Figure 10: Jesus Is Stripped of His Clothes/16
Figure 11: Jesus Is Nailed to the Cross/18
Figure 12: Jesus Dies/19
Figure 13: Jesus Is Taken Down from the Cross/20
Figure 14: Jesus Is Laid in the Tomb/21

Figure 1: Jesus Is Condemned to Death

"When Prometheus was assigned the task of making each of us
    what we are, he put into us something of each other creature in nature."
                                                               —Horace

Only in this way could a human be so utterly believable:
    the perfect curve of marble hands connecting
        supple to supplication.

Here at the first station I was taught
    to watch how Jesus' index and middle finger separate
        from the thumb, point to the sky as Pilate reads.

It is in this way we are blessed.

Caiaphas stands with his hands outstretched
    fingers splayed and downward.

I was taught to see jackals here,
    more than any other creature, the whine and weep
        of packs, how a tongue laps the deep cut
            exposed bone.

Sister Theresa sets her hand on my thigh,
    presses nails into flesh, pushing
        my small knee to the floor.

It is in this way we genuflect
    out of respect; to meditate
        on each prick of thorn and pull of the lash.

I'm 9 years old and I feel less a lion or lamb,
    and more a cobra

I have this hooded heart I can't bear to show.

"This is what suffering looks like," Sister Theresa says.
    It's beautiful.

It stands so perfectly still.

Figure 2: Jesus Takes Up His Cross

The cross sits as the same dull white as the rest
        pigeon-bridge to Jesus' back.

It flowers out like a malignant growth;
        bone spur.

But I see no splinter in the split flesh.
        Smooth as marble.

To my right, Chris continues to fidget, wait
        for Sister Theresa's hand to close around his forearm,
            like she does when she thinks no one is looking.

In this way we both understand
        the grooves between the painted concrete of the bathroom
            walls: something to focus on
                small canoes for our clawing fingers.

She tells him to consider the shoulders
        as only the beginning of the back, withered
            beneath the cut of cat-o-nine-tails.

He considers this as he begins to cry; considers
        as he pulls at his crotch.

The shadow comes quickly to his blue slacks and something
        like warmth drips to the floor.

Piss brings out the maroon of this carpet
        so close to blood
           in temperature and temperament.

Chris would have bled if given the choice.

He would have welcomed the jagged slice over the point
        of curved fingers; laughter in low roar and high pitch.

But we do not choose our torments;

only take on each burden till our scapula cracks
        and the wood sinks in.

We can't see the small bridges
    that buttress us from these things, now
        as we wear the dull and smooth like mantles.

Figure 3: Jesus Falls (1)

It's just my hand on your shoulder
    just a hope, a finger
        indicating direction.

            Why did you fall forward?

Weight distribution, that's all.

No spectral push. No meaning
    larger than exhaustion.

            Stop breathing the dust.

Not souls
    just words of jagged granite
        miners' blood.

            Cough me your name.
            I'll catch it here in my shirt.
            I'll keep it till I wash again.

I'll leave you in the Euphrates with its eponymous tortoise.

He's just like you:
    Soft-shell,
        only semi-aquatic.

            Tell me why I'm here
            and I'll tell you everything

I know about the *gladius, gladiolus:* the little sword,
    prick of its pointed plant.

It's for stabbing;
    single thrust, ribs or below.

Derives its strength from woven strips.

But you already understand the nature of carbon steel;
    friction welds.

            I can see the welts

on your exposed knees
>bone sliver and blood orange.

The two soldiers behind you have dug
>their blades into the soft flesh of your hip,
>>but they won't push you any further down.

They can already see the end of this path.

They know some roads can't help but rise.

Figure 4: Jesus Meets His Mother

This statue isn't marble
    it's ash;
        so much the same except the fire beneath it.

What's ash without fire?

The two figures ask this back and forth,
    but have no answer.

They would stand here forever
    if not for the heat; if not
        for the grasp of the soldier's lash.

"Imagine," Sister Theresa says,
    "this is the last time you see your mother." Imagine

if white hair
    could calm the warlike spirit.

Imagine that I place my index finger on Mary's hooded head
    try to pull the veil back:

all that moves is me.

My mother was always a hooded figure
    her anger ash-like;
        her heart a lingering ember.

The day she left, our driveway turned to dead sea
    more salt than water, where everything I threw in
        refused to sink.

"This is the last time you see her," Sister Theresa said
    but she was wrong.

She'll be there as he waits to die; hidden face
    looking to his hooded heart.

And perhaps they'll see each other.

Though, perhaps, he won't be able
    to take his eyes off the western wall

how Jerusalem slips from the sun; palms
    stand like sentries, while leaves
        wither to spikes.

Their separation from him is a measure of distance.

He prays to this distance.

Figure 5: Simon of Cyrene

So much like his name, Simon listens
    more than carries.

Jesus, with his hands open-palmed, pointed
    to the ground, shows each worn patch of skin.

Simon points a single index finger to the sky,
    proving lift,
        exhibiting the fulcrum,
            this single moment of rest

on which the lever turns and moves
    some body, any body.

This is where I will go:
    up
        when I learn to lift off one knee;

how to grip the smooth and scale
    these marble columns.

Sister Theresa pulls my hands from the statue,
    presses them together in prayer, fingers locked
        and kept from the curved lids of Simon's unpupiled eyes.

Here is the church; here is the steeple.

We show this architecture
    back and forth, how inside us
        there are multitudes

but don't dare uncoil our fingers.

Simon's hands are the only not tied together by ropes;
    not carrying switch or sword.

And so he opens them to whatever might fall
    to the splintered and the split he sees with perfect clarity
        despite his smooth eyes;
            these two dark clouds I couldn't help but touch.

It's always a son who falls, or is about to fall.

Take this burden from me; each of them says.
    Take this heavy wooden rain.

"He chooses this." Sister Theresa says.
    "They ask and he answers."

Such perfect reasoning
    in the soft hum of a drawn sword.

Take this, the metal sings. It belongs to one man no longer.

Figure 6: Veronica Wipes the Face of Jesus

Why are you kneeling?   Why have we both knelt?

Only in this way are we alike
    in stature and statuary.

                       We say drop or fall

when our knees touch
    the ground, like a stone from your palm,

but really we mean pulled
    a common center
        an endless patch of dirt pocked by heels.

This place is smaller than the hairs on a nettle;
    each lonely in their sting and solitude.
        Until now.
                Believe me

when I tell you I've dreamt of this fabric
    a simple swatch of cloth held over a patch of violet flowers,
        their papery bracts.

I think I understand now the worn path, the wine-dark
    of the sage flowers
        that can't help but grow.

Why do I look to their faces after seeing yours?

The oblong leaves;
    these split veins and inflorescent whorls.

                    What I mean to say is
                          you're both beautiful;

what I mean to say is sometimes
    we see a menorah in something as simple as sage.

Figure 7: Jesus Falls (2)

He lays prone on the smooth base,
    with left arm pulled back across his body.

Take this arm, he says,
    this hand.

This plaster cracked down the knucklebone.

It's only symbol,
    symbolon,
        that small thing which has been wrenched apart
            we seek to put back together.
                Desperately.
Such disparity in our desperations.

If I were to compare this broken hand to yours
    if you signed my cast in blood,
        or the wine I stole from the tabernacle,
           would I be healed?

It is in this way we are asked to pretend

to take the body into our mouth
    but not to swallow;
        to taste the blood and believe.

But I don't believe.

This wine-dark liquid has no hand
    on the treacle and spit that filled my mouth after a fight

how it tasted like the snipped tin
    Chris dared me to eat off the floor of my grandfather's shop.

Blood gathers these broken pieces, like sawdust
    spread on bile, and settles them
        into the tender and cursory holes left behind.

It's not that I don't understand how
    different the sound is when the wound is ripped instead of cut;

or how the bruise turns
        from black to red when it breathes.

It's that you fill this cup again
        and again from some glass carafe
                and forget

that no one could ever believe in a blood that tastes so sweet.

Figure 8: The Women of Jerusalem Weep

This hand held out can mean a blessing,
    as in, *my father looks upon you now.*

But it also indicates a stop; the aspirated breath
    at the end of *watch,* and the voiced consonant
        that begins *but come no closer, I have no strength*
to comfort you.

And so he weeps
    to show they are not so different;
        that only a small space separates them

in the same way salt sticks to skin,
    or sun steals water from wood.

These things we carry were once alive,
    though sometimes a cheek is the only proof, sometimes
        the desert can only lead by what is pocked and riven.

He wishes these tears could wash them
    away, pool and churn in white phosphorescence
        till they find themselves on some foreign beach,
            where branches hang lower and looser

in the breeze; a place where men build their boats
    from a single trunk of some strangely named tree:
        royal black or star apple,
            wet and cold even in the midday sun.

He wishes,
    just once,
        to hear the glottal language of a people

who never thought to call their sea *dead.*

Figure 9: Jesus Falls (3)

The sun slides its way through stained-glass robe,
        falls on the right side of the cross brace.

Its red is mutable, moving
        from the bright and incandescent
                to mulled plum; dark as a deep cut.

A long crack in the plaster pulls
        from end to end. Light hangs in the room

like vermilion painted against the Pennsylvania mountains
        I couldn't stop watching on our first family vacation.

I remember how my parents managed to look anywhere
        but at each other; how the path came to linger in its curves,

and how headlights seemed to ignite the olive skin
        of my father's outstretched hand
                as it pointed to constellations along the Milky Way:

Auriga, the charioteer,
        and Perseus, whose bright elbow I first saw
                reflected in my father's glasses.

Less visible is Algol,
        my father said,
                The Ghoul Star, eye of Perseus' prize.

I tried to follow the line of his arm
        through the straight and spin of the road
                till he told me about the Gorgon's stone gaze.

For each constellation after
        I held my thumb against the sky,
                blocking the dark star.

I did not want to succumb to statue,

even as Sister Theresa tries to gather us,
        push us along to the next station.

We can't help but stand sedentary, watching
    the light move along the cross
        as it lies on Jesus' back like a blanket,

like he will lift his head any moment
    and it will slide away.

It looks so simple to escape,
    as if a single breath might split the beam.

But I hold my breath as I run
    my index finger along his sinewy arm. His palm

is flat to the ground, elbow turned
    and caught beneath the weight.

He does not stir.

This object has come to rest.

Figure 10: Jesus Is Stripped of His Clothes

It's a difference in focus
       how the eyes relax, take in the visible,
              but have no specific attention.

It's a question of aspect, area; how much
       of the sea one can see in winter;

how it seems that snow can crop the sand; water
       can hang off ice like a blanket draped
             above the clavicle, translucent, tight
                    as plaster cloth caught mid-fall on Jesus' torso.

This is still life,

the angle and slope
       of each torn section. Arms outstretched.

The arms are always outstretched,
       and so we pay no mind to this.

Instead we watch the eyes,
       wish we could paint the irides
             some bright and unexpected color.

My eyes are red most mornings, the tear
       and scratch through hallways; broken lines
             and the binary code of affection.

Chris clasps his hands
       in prayer, forms them into a ball,
             and so claims the zero.

I stand against the marble column, pretend
       to be a one; singular and straight in posture.

We form a simple switch; a thing
       that can only exist in two states, on or off.

One must necessarily be
       because the other is not.

He is not, his hands claim, as do his eyes,
> though these things are always changing.

Soon we will shuffle off, forget
> the angle of embarrassment we find in this corner;
>> walk briskly on our separate paths from the schoolyard,

hiding what is secret; both
> hoping the brush might rend a button or hem

and leave its jagged licks on the flesh below.

Figure 11: Jesus Is Nailed to the Cross

There's something I haven't told you:
    that a hand may curl around a wrist, or a neck;

that this is how I was led
    to believe
        to be in such places.

And though I forget the feel
    of some dark corner of desk,
        or how the shade fell from room to room,

I can still hear the water as it ran
    each morning like kite string:
        pulled from tangle and sudden tug.

I can remember this:
    a hand may be cold
        more claw than caress. A small nail

still sticks to the plaster,
    the open palm. A hammer

falls but does not connect.

The hammer is always falling,
    and so this is a perfect admission:
        an act of letting in.

The Latin licked like silver pieces;
    the clothing pared.

When we do not understand we close our eyes,
    learn to hold our breath.

We count as instructed.

When we finally let go, what breath we have circles
    like Sirocco, storm of the southeastern winds,
        where the faithful dream of dust, and whispers

hang in the air like tiny spheres of prayer.

Figure 12: Jesus Dies

There's such weight to be held by the hands;
>volume of the chest's cylinder.

Barbet said of crucifixion
>that if the arms were pulled back to such an angle,
>>the hyperextension would move from deltoids to
>>>pectorals, and pull each breath in tighter, faster.

This is an argument about space:

how far Mary stands from the cross base; how little air
>is necessary to continue breathing;
>>how much of it smells of dried blood.

Sister Theresa doesn't have to ask for silence here.

Each of us stands with hands in pockets,
>trying to reach further than the cloth's catch.

I know we are looking at death
>because the head hangs forward;
>>eyes closed.

And that's what death is supposed to look like:
>clean in its plaster cast, the crown of thorns
>>only seconds from slipping.

But within this there are memories, whole days
>of silence I thought had been picked clean, only to find
>>them illuminated again by the single barb of sunbeam
>>>that slips through a collar or a rolled cuff:

simple letters tacked above his head,
>*INRI,* that I didn't ask about, or understand as shorthand.

I mouthed them again and again, trying
>to find some secret word; an incantation in the breath;

simple song that waits and swells the tongue.

Figure 13: Jesus Is Taken Down from the Cross

A single man struggles on a crude ladder,
    only 4 rungs, poorly spaced.

Chris runs his fingers along the molded plaster ropes
    that seem to just barely hold everything together.

The cord is finely edged,
    double knotted; rounded like a basilic vein,
        wrapping each fixture as if it were a forearm.

It looks as though any step up or down
    would collapse the entire structure;
        scaffolding bent and sunken.

The man's two fingers seem to support
    the whole body, grafted by brushstroke,
        flesh-colored paint that swirls through the shoulder.

The body hangs in the air like a magic trick: chair
    balanced on a single digit, perfect placement, singular miracle
        buried
            in doubt and disparity between mass and weight.

We don't want to believe
    it's about direction, even in removal
        even in loss.

Jesus' fingers point downward along the Y-axis,
    create the creased line of his mother's face, her forearms

outstretched as support beams,
    sharp in their angles,

ready to bear all that's been given.

Figure 14: Jesus Is Laid in the Tomb

It's silent in the nave, with its columns
    of identical wooden pews,

and this long quiet is rounded
    like the bow of a ship, its namesake ark;
        twin lighthouses of open vestibule doors.

We are tired sailors
    following the mourning dove,

with Chris as helmsman, his smile
    an assurance against waiting rocks.

The doors click shut; the sudden
    slope of a boulder, and the chamber becomes hollow,
        dark, a reliquary,
            waiting for what is blessed to be interred.

By itself it's just an object of space,
    four sides standing
        smooth to the touch.

But Sister Theresa has told us the story a dozen times:

how push or pull could never have moved it
    how impossible the raw strength.

Calculate the coefficient of friction,
    stone on stone; believe
        an object at rest tends to stay at rest.

We name stars on starless nights
    because we remember their light, and we call this faith:

how difficult the balance on its first step.

We walk into the night air,
    inhale some hidden light, speak
        to those we love, and call this passion:

how bitter its etymology; how tangled its root.